The Jesse Owens Story

by Gabi Mezger

COVER-TO-COVER BOOKS

Perfection Learning®

Inside Illustration: Kay Ewald

Dedication

To my mother, Lotte Mezger,
whose skill with languages has always inspired me

About the Author

Gabi Mezger has taught Hebrew, Jewish studies, and
music to a generation of students of all ages. She has
previously written educational materials in her native
language, Hebrew. This is her first book in English.

Gabi Mezger is currently a singer and a songwriter,
working as part of a team called Yad B'Yad with storyteller
Katy Z. Allen. Together they write, perform, and record
original songs and stories for children and adults.

Gabi Mezger grew up in Israel. She now lives in
Massachusetts.

For information, contact
Perfection Learning® Corporation,
1000 North Second Avenue, P.O. Box 500,
Logan, Iowa 51546-1099.
Paperback ISBN 0-7891-2002-x
Cover Craft® ISBN 0-7807-6690-3

Table of Contents

Chapter 1

Hello, World!
Here I Am

"It's a boy!"

The tiny new baby had a big name. His name was James Cleveland Owens. His name was too big for him. So his parents called him J. C. for short.

J. C. was born in Alabama on September 12, 1913. He was the youngest of nine brothers and sisters.

The Owens family didn't have much money. But they had fun. In summer, they swam and fished. They made campfires at night.

An Alabama school for black
children in the early 1900s

J. C. went to school. But the school was only for black children. The teacher did not get paid. Many days, the teacher wasn't there. J. C. didn't learn much.

J. C. was nine. The family moved to Cleveland, Ohio. He went to a new school.

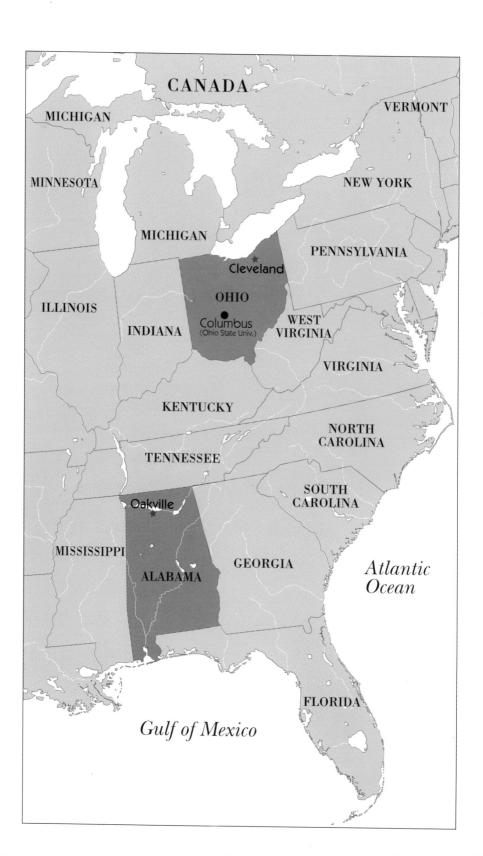

"What's your name?" asked the teacher.

"J. C. Owens."

J. C. had grown up in the South. He had a strong accent. The teacher couldn't understand him.

"Jesse?" asked the teacher.

"Yes," J. C. answered. "J. C. Owens."

"OK, Jesse," said the teacher. "Welcome to our class." From then on, J. C. was Jesse.

J. C. had missed too much school. He could not read or write. He was put into first grade. Jesse was older than everyone.

But Jesse went to school every day. He learned to read and write. Soon he moved into second grade. He was happy. But he was still the oldest student.

1896	1900	1904	1908	1912	1916	1920
First Modern Olympics are held in Greece 1896				Jesse Owens is born 1913	World War I begins 1914	World War I ends 1918	Owens family moves to Cleveland 1922

2 Chapter

As Fast as the Wind

Jesse liked to run. He ran like the wind. In junior high school, he ran many races.

Jesse also liked the high jump and the long jump. He jumped in track meets.

Charles Riley was Jesse's track coach. He taught Jesse to run faster and jump higher and longer.

Charles Riley

Jesse ready to run in the AAU Track and
Field Championships. He won the 100-m final
in world-record time of 10.3 seconds.

Bettmann

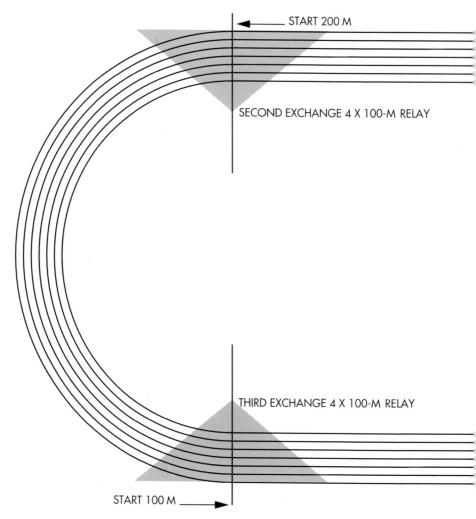

START 200 M

SECOND EXCHANGE 4 X 100-M RELAY

THIRD EXCHANGE 4 X 100-M RELAY

START 100 M

Track layout with starting lines and finish for running events

Jesse was handsome. He was also friendly, but shy. Everyone liked him.

Two friends liked to watch Jesse run. One was Ruth Solomon. She was

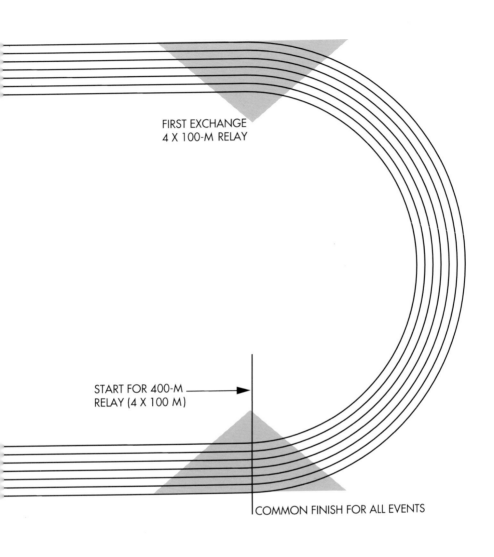

FIRST EXCHANGE
4 X 100-M RELAY

START FOR 400-M
RELAY (4 X 100 M)

COMMON FINISH FOR ALL EVENTS

two years younger than Jesse. The other was David Albritton. He also liked sports. Ruth and David were Jesse's best friends.

When Jesse was 15 years old, he jumped 6 feet in the high jump. He jumped almost 23 feet in the long jump. No one his age had ever jumped so high or so far. Jesse set two world records.

In high school, Jesse ran in 79 races. He won 75 of them.

Then Jesse went to a big track meet in Chicago. Only the best runners and jumpers were there. Track stars came from all over the United States.

Jesse's team earned 54 points. Jesse earned 30 of them! And he broke another world record.

Jesse went home to Cleveland. The city honored him with a big parade. Everyone cheered for Jesse.

Jesse performing long jump in Chicago meet

Bettmann

1928	1929	1930	1931	1932	1933	
Jesse enters Fairmount Junior High School 1928	Jesse sets his first record in the long jump (22 ft 11¾ in) 1928	Jesse enters East Technical High School 1930		Jesse graduates from high school 1933	Jesse sets world record in the 220-yard dash (20.7 sec) 1933	Jesse ties the world record in the 100-yard dash (9.4 sec) 1933

Chapter 3

More Broken Records

Jesse was 19 years old. He had just finished high school. And he was going to college! He would go to Ohio State.

Jesse wanted to run in college meets. He was good enough. But it was his first year in college. And he was not old enough.

Jesse and a friend working in
the Ohio State Senate in 1935

OSU Photo Archives

Jesse entered other track meets.
These meets were open to everyone.
Jesse won many races. And he broke
many world records.

Jesse with Ohio State
head track coach Larry Snyder

OSU Photo Archives

Once, Jesse raced with three other men. One of the men slipped. He couldn't finish. Jesse won the race.

Jesse saw what happened. "We'll run the race again," he said. They did.

This time his friend won. But the crowd honored Jesse for his fair play.

During college, Jesse got married. He married his high school friend, Ruth Solomon.

Jesse and Ruth at Ohio State Homecoming football game in 1936

OSU Photo Archives

1933	1934		1935		
Jesse enters Ohio State University 1933	Jesse sets state and conference records in all events 1934	Hitler organizes the German army 1935	Jesse breaks world records in the long jump (26 ft 8¼ in) and the 220-yard sprint (20.3 sec) 1935	Jesse ties world record in the 100-yard dash (9.4 sec) 1935	Jesse marries Ruth Solomon 1935

Adolf Hitler

Chapter 4

To Go or Not to Go?

The 1936 Olympics were in Berlin. Berlin is in Germany.

Bad things were happening in Germany. Adolf Hitler was in power.

He did not like Jews. He didn't like nonwhites either. He made many new laws. These laws were bad for Jews and nonwhites.

Many people were angry. They didn't like Hitler. They didn't like the way he treated Jews.

EUROPE
IN 1936

Sweden
Finland
Norway
North
Sea
Estonia
Ireland
Denmark
Latvia
Great
Baltic
Britain
Netherlands
Sea
Lithuania
Berlin
East
Prussia
Soviet Union
Atlantic
Ocean
Belgium
Germany
Luxembourg
Poland
France
Czechoslovakia
Switzerland
Austria
Hungary
Romania
Portugal
Yugoslavia
Spain
Italy
Black Sea
Bulgaria
Albania
Spanish Morocco
Greece
Mediterranean Sea
Turkey
Morocco
Algeria
Tunisia
Cyprus

Some people didn't want the U.S.
team to go to Germany. They didn't
want to honor Hitler.

Jesse wanted to go to the Games.
He trained every day. He wanted to
win.

Jews and Christians worked together. They protested. They tried to keep the team home. But at last, it was decided. The team would go to the Games!

The team crossed the ocean on a big ship. In Berlin, Jesse met many people. They had come from all over the world. Jesse liked meeting so many different people.

1935				1936	
Members of Olympic committee visit Germany to evaluate Nazi policies 1935	Press urges a boycott of the Olympics by the American athletes 1935	AAU decides to send athletes to the Olympics 1935	Jesse continues to set new records 1936	The Olympic team sails for Europe 1936	The Olympiad XI opens in Berlin 1936

Chapter 5

Hitler's Grandest Day

It was August 1, 1936. The Games opened. Hitler was proud and happy.

In the afternoon, there was a big parade. First came Hitler. He stood in his big open car. He wore an army uniform.

Behind him came the German team. They were all white and all Christian. No one was black or Jewish.

Hitler wished that all world team members were white. Many of them were. But many, like Jesse, were not.

Jewish and black team members marched in the parade. Hispanics marched too. So did Arabs and Asians.

Hitler hated them all. He hated some because they were not white. He hated others because they were not Christian.

But Hitler wasn't worried. He knew his team would win. "They will show the world," he said. "They will prove that white people are better than others."

The opening ceremonies of the 1936 Olympics

Chapter 6

The Olympics—My Goal!

The Games began. Jesse's teammates were ready. But Jesse wasn't.

Jesse had lost his new shoes on the ship. He looked for them everywhere. He could not find them. The shoes were gone.

A friend looked for a new pair of shoes. He looked all over Berlin. He searched and searched.

Jesse (far right) and teammates huddle in
blankets after running the 100-m dash at the Games.

It was Jesse's turn to run. Finally,
the friend found a pair of shoes. Jesse

put them on. They hurt his feet. But
he had no choice.

Jesse jumped in his new shoes. And he jumped farther than anyone else.

Jesse ran too. He ran faster than anyone else. He set many records.

Jesse won four gold medals. He won gold medals in the 100-meter dash and the 200-meter dash. He won the long jump. And he won the 400-meter relay.

Jesse (far left) and members of the U.S. 400-m relay team

Jesse on the winners' stand after winning
the long jump. Luz Long is standing behind him.

Bettmann

Luz Long was a member of the German team. He competed against Jesse in the long jump.

After Jesse won, Luz shook hands with Jesse. They became friends.

Jesse proudly displaying three of his four gold medals

Bettmann

34

Jesse (top right) crossing
the finish line in the 100-m dash

Bettmann

The band played four times for Jesse. The crowd cheered for Jesse Owens.

Jesse had proven Hitler wrong. The people were happy. And Jesse was proud.

1936

| Jesse ties the world record in the 100-m dash (10.3 sec) 1936 | Jesse sets an Olympic record in the long jump (26 ft 5¼ in) 1936 | Jesse sets an Olympic record in the 200-m sprint (20.7 sec) 1936 | Jesse leads 400-m relay team to a world and an Olympic record (39.8 sec) 1936 | Olympics close. Olympic grounds become training centers for Nazi troops 1936 |

Jesse boarding a train shortly
after his return from the Olympics

OSU Photo Archives

Chapter 7

After the Olympics

After the Games, Jesse ran in meets in Europe. Crowds of people were everywhere. Everyone wanted to meet Jesse. They wanted his autograph.

Jesse signing autographs for fans   OSU Photo Archives

Jesse and Larry Snyder in a victory parade   OSU Photo Archives

But Jesse was tired and homesick. So he came home early. He lived with his wife Ruth. They had three daughters.

After coming home, Jesse looked for work. He tried many things. He opened a dry cleaning store. Later, he owned a basketball team and a softball team.

Jesse also worked for Ford Motor Company. He found better housing for workers. He helped solve problems of black families.

Jesse also worked for the New York Mets baseball team. He was the team's running coach.

Jesse working as an assistant track coach at Ohio State University

OSU Photo Archives

Jesse and Ruth with daughter Marlene,
the 1960 Ohio State Homecoming Queen

In 1950, Jesse Owens received an honor. He was named the best track-and-field athlete ever.

Jesse died of cancer in 1980.

1936	1936	1937	1938	1938	1939	1943	1945	1950	1980
Jesse tours Europe with Olympians 1936	Jesse becomes homesick and returns 1936	Jesse organizes a touring basketball team 1937	Jesse organizes a touring softball team 1938	Jesse opens a dry cleaning company 1938	World War II begins 1939	Jesse begins work with Ford Motor Company 1943	World War II ends 1945	Jesse named greatest track athlete of the past century 1950	Jesse Owen dies of lun cancer 1980

Jesse in 1978. He died two years later of lung cancer.   OSU Photo Archives

Chapter

The First Olympics

The Games began a long time ago. Before Jesse Owens was born. The first Games were held more than 2,700 years ago!

These Games were held in Greece. Greece is a small country in Europe.

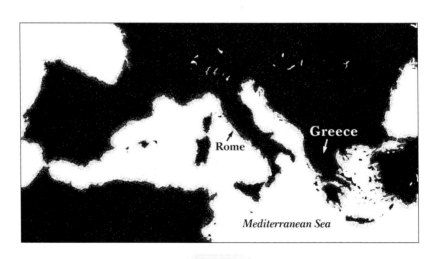

Vase painting of short distance
runners in the first Olympics

Bettmann

But the Games were not like the Games today. There wasn't any basketball or ice-skating.

Women didn't play. In fact, they couldn't even watch!

Every four years, men came together in the Stadium of Olympia. They ran short races against each other.

The winners were given crowns of olive leaves. And no one ever got his picture on a box of cereal!

Years later, longer races were added. So were wrestling and chariot races.

Many years later, Rome ruled Greece. The Games didn't mean as much. One ruler finally ordered an end to them. There weren't any Games for more than 1,500 years.

Ruins of the Stadium of Olympia

Chapter 9

The Modern Olympics

In 1875, the ruins of the Stadium of Olympia were found. The ruins gave a French teacher an idea. He was Pierre de Coubertin.

He thought the Games should begin again. Pierre hoped that every country would send a team.

In 1894, Pierre presented his idea to a sports group. They voted to start the International Olympic Committee.

King of Greece presenting awards
at first modern Olympics in 1896

Bettmann

The first modern Games took place
in 1896. They were held in Greece.
Just like the old Games.

46

Baron Pierre de Coubertin, founder
of the modern Olympics

Bettmann

Winners received medals instead of crowns. First place received a gold medal. Second place was given a silver medal. And third place was given a bronze medal.

Everyone liked the Games. In 1900, Paris hosted the Games. Women entered several events for the first time.

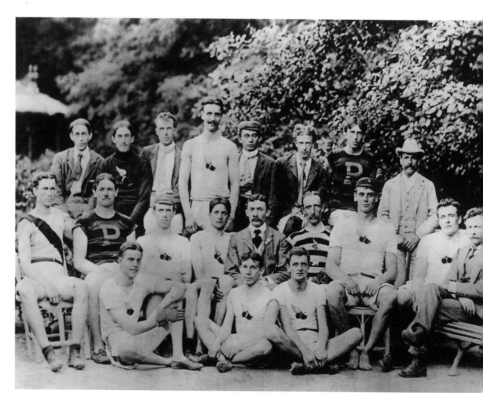

1900 U.S. Olympic team

Bettmann

The Winter Games started in 1924   Bettmann

Women proved that they could play sports too. They ran, jumped, and swam. Now there are almost as many women as men at the Olympics.

In 1924, the Winter Games started. They had ice-skating, skiing, and other winter sports.

The Games have been held every four years since 1896. They were called off only three times—1916, 1940, and 1944. That was because of World Wars I and II.

The 1936 Games were not the only ones to have problems. Many teams stayed away from the Games in the 1970s and the 1980s. Teams didn't agree with some ideas of the host countries.

Hitler is gone now. So is Jesse Owens. The Games still take place.

Teams come from many countries. They look different. They speak different languages. But they are all Olympians. They all believe in themselves. They are all winners.

Chapter 10

The Future Olympics

Many things have changed since Jesse Owens was in the Games. Runners seem to run faster. Jumpers jump higher and longer.

In the first modern Games, some runners wore street shoes. Those shoes had hard, slick soles. The shoes didn't bend easily.

The runners ran on bumpy, cinder tracks. The loose cinders made running hard.

Cinder

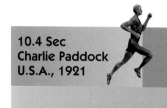

10.4 Sec
Charlie Paddock
U.S.A., 1921

10.2 Sec
Jesse Owens
U.S.A., 1936

10.1 Sec
Willie Williams
U.S.A., 1956

This chart shows 8 famous 100-meter runners from the past 75 years.

During the early modern Games, the runners' clothes were baggy and heavy.

Today, runners have shoes made for them. Shoemakers make a mold of the

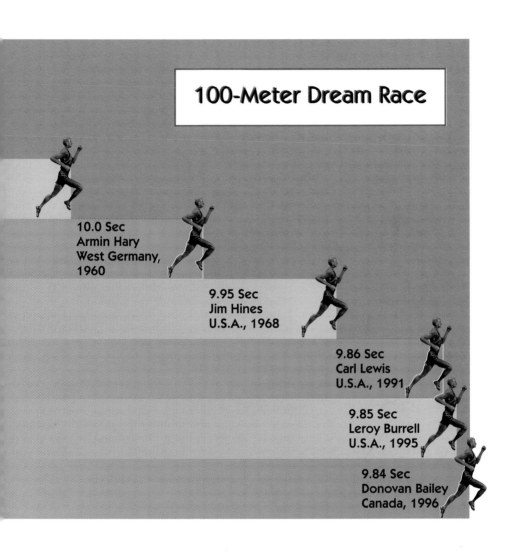

100-Meter Dream Race

10.0 Sec
Armin Hary
West Germany,
1960

9.95 Sec
Jim Hines
U.S.A., 1968

9.86 Sec
Carl Lewis
U.S.A., 1991

9.85 Sec
Leroy Burrell
U.S.A., 1995

9.84 Sec
Donovan Bailey
Canada, 1996

runner's foot. Then they make a lightweight shoe from the mold.

Tracks are often made of rubber. The runner's shoes don't slip. Therefore, the runner can run faster!

Clothes are made of lightweight cloth. The clothes hug the runner's body. They don't flap in the wind and slow the runner down.

Jesse's trainers had to look at newsreels to see how he ran. They told Jesse what to do or change. Then Jesse would run faster and jump higher.

Today, doctors study the body and how it works. They use computers to study how people run and jump. They hope to help runners.

Pierre de Coubertin made a motto for the first modern Games. It was *Faster, Higher, Stronger.*

OSU Photo Archives

He had a dream. He didn't want athletes to settle for a record. He wanted them to try to be better.

What will happen in the future? Will records continue to be broken? How fast will athletes run in the future? Will they fulfill Pierre's dream?

Look for these other
Cover-to-Cover chapter books!

The Elephant's Ancestors

Great Eagle and Small One

James Meets the Prairie

Little Fish

Magic Tricks and More

What If You'd Been at Jamestown?

What's New with Mr. Pizooti?

The Whooping Crane

Yankee Doodle and the Secret Society